Friendship Forever

The All About You Guide to the Friends in Your Life

By Lia Haberman

allabout**YOU!**

SCHOLASTIC INC.
New York Toronto London Auckland Sydney
Mexico City New Delhi Hong Kong

This book is dedicated to all my favorite girl-friends in Montreal, New York, London, and Los Angeles, and to my husband, Todd.

Thanks to Roxanne Camron, Beth Mayall, and Sara Fiedelholtz.

Cover photos by Jon McKee.

ISBN 0-439-06276-4

12 11 10 9 8 7 6 5 4 3   9/9 0 1 2 3 4/0

Printed in the U.S.A.
First Scholastic printing, April 1999

Contents

Introduction

All About This Book

You probably spend more time with your friends than with just about anyone else — except maybe your family. You sit with them on the school bus and next to them in class all day. You eat lunch together and hang out after school and on weekends. A friend might drive you crazy sometimes (how *could* she have dropped your favorite novel in the bathtub!) but you gotta admit, friends make each and every day more fun.

Whether you want to make more friends, become a better friend, or bring a friendship to an end, this book is for you. Even if you've got a great friend and you think you know every single detail about her life, check out Chapter Six — there's always more to learn!

Thing is, you only get as much out of a friendship as you put into it. If you're only a so-so pal then you'll probably be disappointed over and over again by the people you call friends. But be the best friend you can be and you'll never be lonely again. So sympathize when your friend complains about her wacky family (even if you think her folks are great). Don't forget to call her after her swim meet to see how she did and NEVER forget to send her postcards or e-mail when you go on vacation. The payoff will be a true-blue friend who'll stick with you through thick and thin.

Chapter One
All About Us

There are scrapbooks to record a baby's first words or a couple's wedding vows, but who keeps track of friendship memories? With this book now you can! Use these pages to write in all you can remember about meeting your best friend (or best friends if you've got more than one). If you forget some of the details, ask your pal if she can help you fill in the blanks. Not only will you be preserving your best friendship moments, you may even grow closer as you share your memories.

Answer the following questions in the space provided (or you can create a separate book or journal to record your memories).

How did you meet?

_____

_____

_____

Where did you meet?

_____

_____

_____

Were you friends at first sight?

_____

_____

_____

What's your favorite thing to do together?

_____

_____

_____

How are you alike?

_____

_____

_____

How are you different?

_____

_____

_____

How has your friend changed your life?

_____

_____

_____

What's the best advice your friend has ever given you?

_____

_____

_____

Do you share a special code language no one else knows?

_____

_____

_____

What's the coolest thing the two of you have ever done together?

_____

_____

_____

What's the toughest experience you've ever been through together?

_____

_____

_____

When was your best sleepover of all time?

_____

_____

_____

What do you know about her that no one else knows?

_____

_____

_____

What deep, dark secret does she know about you?

_____

_____

_____

What could you spend hours doing together?

_____

_____

_____

Chapter Two
New Kid on the Block

Or How to Make New Friends

"**M**y older sister has already moved away from home and my best friend since kindergarten is moving as soon as her parents sell their house. I cry about this every single day."

Ashley, Pennsylvania

Maybe you've just moved to a new city, maybe you're trying to change the circle of friends you have right now, or maybe your best friend just moved away. Basically, being without friends is no fun. So where do you start? Look around you. Is there a girl in your class with whom you have something in common? Or maybe there's someone you admire from afar, like the goalie of the girl's soccer team?

The more you and your potential pal have to talk about, the more your friendship will have going for it. Deciding you're going to become best friends with the most popular girl in the class might seem like a fun idea at the time, but without any common interests, your friendship just isn't going to last. As much as you like them, true friends should be kids who think you're as cool as you think they are.

Once you've met someone you think you might really click with, how do you determine if this person is true bud material? Here are some telltale signs:

- You look forward to spending time with her.
- You like yourself when you're around her because she brings out the best in you.
- You don't feel nervous or anxious to please when you're with her.

Get the ball rolling
Let's say you've set your sights on becoming friends with the girl who sits next to you in English class (you both love spooky stories) —

what do you do now? It sounds obvious but a simple hello really is your best bet. Then you can talk about your mutual interest. Ask her if she's read the latest book in a popular horror series or find out if she likes the same authors that you do.

Most people are flattered when others take an interest in them. Making the jump from classmates to friends won't take long if you're genuinely interested in getting to know her. Maybe you could offer to lend her your favorite book, ask if you can join her during recess, or invite her over to watch a movie after school.

Here are some suggestions on how you can meet new friends:

- Join the drama club, the track team, or the chorus at school where you'll meet like-minded kids.
- Bring a conversation starter to school. Pass around a postcard from your pen pal, pictures of your puppy, or a cool necklace you beaded — anything to get people talking. Just don't bring it out during the middle of class! Once you're all talking,

it'll be easy to figure out who you think would make a good friend.

- If you're a reader, find out if your school has a book club or reading group. If not, ask the librarian if you can start one. Members could get together once a week during lunch or after school to talk about the best book they've read recently or a book they've all agreed to read. It'll give you the chance to meet people who share one of your passions — books!

- Sign up for every activity, volunteer group, and bake sale you can. You'll earn respect as the girl who gets stuff done and meet new people along the way.

- Expand your horizons and get to know kids outside of school, too. For instance, find out if your local museum offers classes for kids after school or on the weekend or sign up for lifeguarding lessons at the municipal pool.

- Get yourself in the friendship groove by getting in touch with an old friend. It can be anyone from a camp roomie to the neighbor who moved away. She might be able to introduce you to her friends or just remind you that you *are* a person others *want* to be friends with and that you can be loads of fun.

- Be the type of person you'd like to get to know. Have a friendly smile ready for everyone and something nice to say when others talk to you. You just might be surprised how many people smile back.

Help for the tongue-tied

You'd love to try and make new friends if only you were confident that when you opened your mouth something stupid wouldn't pop out. Would you believe looking or sounding dumb is something everyone, from your parents to the most popular kid in school, worries about? But it shouldn't stop you from having the circle of friends you want and being as social as you want to be.

The next time you have a conversation with someone you'd like to get to know, spend less time worrying about what type of impression you're making. Since most people love to talk about themselves, if you're genuinely interested in listening, your friend-to-be will most likely end up doing most of the talking. It'll take the pressure off you. So just start by asking your potential bud how she is or what she's doing this weekend. It might seem tough to get the words out at first, but it gets easier with practice, and considering the lonely alternative, you've got nothing to lose.

Keep the following cues in mind the next time you're gabbing with a potential friend:

- Speak clearly and avoid using expressions like "uh" and "um."
- Maintain eye contact with a new friend so that you seem interested in the conversation. But don't get into a staring match — you might end up scaring her off.
- Be aware of her body language. If she's got somewhere to go, she'll be especially grateful that you picked up on her restless signals. Suggest continuing the conversation at another time.
- Respond to what she's saying. If she's telling you about her sister getting sick and you're thinking about something funny instead, the smile on your face may give her the impression that you're either a space cadet or you really don't care.
- Don't abruptly change the subject or start bragging about yourself while she's talking. It'll either make you come across as completely uninterested in what she's saying

or else you'll seem conceited and self-absorbed — and no one wants to be friends with someone like that!

But I want to be best friends!
"My best friend always listens to me and helps me out. She's so understanding and easygoing even when I freak out about things. She's helped me to become a better person."

Kate, Oregon

Wouldn't you love to have — or be — a friend like that? You can. But don't rush things even if you think your new friend is the coolest person you've ever met.

True friendship takes time and care. You have to hang in there day after day even when times are tough. So if you're wondering what it takes to become someone's best friend, here's your answer: It takes interest, under-standing, patience, and the ability to forgive. Listen to her stories, sympathize with her problems, and don't give up on her when she messes up or hurts your feelings. Your bond won't happen overnight. You'll have to build your relationship to the point where she knows she can trust you — and where you know you can trust her, too. Then you might truly be best friends.

What if nobody likes me?

Ashley had a terrible day. Her best friend, Amy, was out sick so she had no one to share lunch with. Then when the teacher asked everyone to get into groups, no one asked Ashley to join their group. After school Ashley walked home alone since it didn't seem like the other girls who lived in her neighborhood wanted her company. She went to bed feeling miserable and lonely. She realized that if her best friend ever moved away she'd be completely alone!

Everyone has days when they feel alone. But you can change things. For example, Ashley could've joined one of the groups herself but didn't feel like making the effort. And the girls who didn't seem interested in talking to her on their way home? Since Ashley usually ignored them to walk with Amy, can you blame them for not rushing to Ashley's side the one day her best friend wasn't there?

With a positive attitude, Ashley's day could've been a lot different. If you ever find yourself in a similar situation, stop and think about it.

It's actually pretty unlikely that *everyone* dislikes you. A lot of people probably don't even know anything about you, so how could they dislike you? But don't wait around for them to discover how wonderful you are. It's your job to let others know you're a cool person and that you would be a good friend. And that means being friendly, open, and accepting — and not just when your best friend is absent!

They *really* don't like me

"There's a bunch of kids at school who don't like me. They whisper about me behind my back and they're always laughing at me. I don't know what I did to make them hate me so much. They really make my life hard sometimes."

Lisa, New York

Unfortunately, sometimes matters are out of your hands. For example, if someone starts a nasty rumor about you being stuck-up, which causes other kids to be wary of you, it's not your fault — bad things happen to good people. Some kids are just plain mean. It's possible they may dislike you for no real reason at all. Sometimes kids end up bonding over the fact that they all don't like a particular person. It isn't fair if you end up being that person, but you're just going to have to accept the fact that you can't be friends with everyone.

However, if someone *is* making your life miserable by spreading rumors about you, tell your close friend or friends how badly you feel. Your true friends will be able to separate fact from fiction and will stand up for you when people say untrue things about you. If you do know who started the rumor, quietly and calmly confront them. Don't scream or threaten them because this will only make the situation worse. And don't start rumors about them to retaliate because then the feud will never end. Instead, tell them their info is wrong and ask them to please stop gossiping about you.

If the situation gets out of control and none of your friends seems to be able to help, talk to a counselor or an adult you trust. She might be able to shed some light on the situation or explain things in a way that your friends can't. Your teacher might be the one who realizes that the girl who started the rumors is actually jealous of you for some reason (maybe because of how well you did on your oral presentation) and that's why she's dishing the dirt. There are some kids to whom you might never be close but you shouldn't have to feel like you're going off to battle when you leave for school every morning! So don't let people get away with spreading rumors about you. But also don't be too disappointed if not *everyone* wants to be your friend — after all, you don't need to be friendly with everyone to have some very good friendships.

How we became best friends . . .

Some friends hit it off the moment they meet, as if it were only a matter of time before fate brought them together. Here are a few stories about some instant best buds:

"I knew my best bud and I would be BFF when we started to talk in homeroom. We discovered we had everything in common. We're both totally psychic and can predict things and we have the same taste in stuff."

Ryan, Massachusetts

"In fourth grade, one of my best friends bailed to hang with 'cooler' people, so I started hanging with a new girl and we became inseparable. We went everywhere together. I didn't even have time to miss my old friend."

Denise, California

"I was in second grade and this one boy in fifth grade liked to pick on me and another girl. She and I would sit in the corner and cry and try to convince each other that everything would be OK. That's when I realized she really cared."

Katy, Florida

"I was new in school and didn't know anyone when a girl came up and said, 'Hi, my name's Tara. What's yours?' It turned out to be one of the boldest things Tara ever did because she's really shy but it worked and we've been best friends ever since."

Giuliana, Toronto, Canada

"My mom made me take swimming lessons all summer long. I met my best friend in the deep end of the pool. Her mom was making her go every morning, too. Soon we had each other laughing so hard the water didn't seem as cold. I couldn't have made it through the summer without her."

Lisa, New York

"I was tall for my age and always had to sit at the back of the class so I wouldn't obstruct other people's view of the teacher or the blackboard. My height made me very self-conscious until an even taller girl joined our class and sat next to me. Finally, someone I had something in common with! This encouraged me to try being friends with others who were like me — more shy and bookish than popularity queen. I discovered I had a lot in common with a bunch of people."

Ann, Washington

Sometimes friendships don't start out quite as smoothly. Check out these friends who almost didn't connect but then ended up clicking:

"Other friends had warned me that the new girl was totally obnoxious and stubborn. But after meeting her I realized she was just superindependent and refused to follow people just to be popular. I really admired her spirit and we've been friends ever since."

Amy, New York

"I was in gymnastics class when this new girl joined. She was really good, better than any of us there. Because of that, most of us couldn't stand her and thought she was a show-off. One day she asked me why we hated her. She was so genuine and really wanted to be liked, I felt awful. Her honesty turned me into her biggest fan."

Jane, Ohio

"I was working on a group project at school with one girl and a bunch of boys. She seemed like a real snob because she always avoided being alone with me. As I got to know her I realized she was just painfully shy and we finally worked past that to become friends."

Carol, Florida

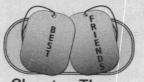

Chapter Three

How to Be a (Best) Friend

Friendship is sort of like a plant — care for it and it'll keep growing and getting stronger, but forget to water it and it will wilt. You can't just assume that seeing your friend at school every day will guarantee a long-lasting friendship. You've got to put some work into it. You know, cheer her up when she's down, forgive her when she messes up, and support her when she's doing really well (even when you're not).

So read the following tips and then try to put them into practice for the next few weeks. It'll only take a little extra effort to strengthen the friendships you already have. And who knows, you might even find yourself becoming better friends with someone you didn't expect to click with.

Listen up

"She always listens when I have a problem, instead of trying to solve it for me. She cries along with me till there aren't any tears left and there's nothing more to say. She'll sit with me till I'm ready to face the world again with a smile. And chances are, she helped put that smile on my face."

Kate, Oregon

Say your friend's describing the awful fight she had with her parents last night and it reminds you of the megabattle you had with your mom last week and you decide you just have to share it with her — *now*. Well, resist the urge and keep your mouth shut. There are times when putting in your two cents is fine, but other times it's best to just listen to a friend spill her guts without interrupting.

Being genuinely interested in what your friends have to say shows you care more than any Hallmark card you could ever send. Besides, you won't learn anything about other people if all you do is listen to yourself talk. If you insist on blabbing every time your friend opens her mouth, she'll soon turn to someone else's more welcoming ear when she's got something important to say.

21

If you've been making the mistake of continually interrupting your friend whenever she's speaking, it's not too late to make up for it. Call up your pal and ask what's on her mind — then shut up and listen! It might take a while to regain her trust, but your friend will begin to open up again once she knows she has your attention and interest.

Be a support system

Lisa didn't really understand why her best friend Carol liked playing the viola so much. There was all that practicing and, besides, Lisa thought there were a lot of other instruments that sounded much nicer. But every time Carol played a concert, Lisa showed up and clapped louder than anyone else.

Even if you don't share your friend's dedication to saving the rain forests, her obsession with college basketball, or her love of rap music, you can still support her in all her interests and be her number-one fan. Imagine how good she'll feel when you remember she's racing in a track meet and wish her good luck — or if you show up to cheer her on!

It doesn't take all that much effort on your part to make your friend feel great. And when you make her feel wonderful about herself she'll probably do the same for you.

Of course, boosting your friend's ego is a whole lot easier when you've got nothing at stake — but it's just as important to pump her up even if you're both competing for the same thing or when you're feeling down and need some support yourself. So when she makes the debate team and you don't, you need to just grin and bear it. It'll be to your credit because it takes a really strong person to be happy for her friend's success.

Keep it in the vault

"I knew we were BFFs when I told her my most sacred secret and she kept it to herself and told no one."

Alison, Virginia

A good friend is someone who knows she's been trusted with something special when you tell her a secret. After all, why would you share your deepest thoughts if you believed they'd just end up being spread around the school? A good friend knows this and can be depended on to keep your confidences.

Unfortunately, some people see sharing secrets as a means to becoming more popular with others. Momentarily, gossip has the effect of getting everyone's interest and making the person telling it the center of attention. Many people are tempted by attention and gossip for this reason. Problem is, once a secret's been told, it can never be taken back. And by telling secrets that have been entrusted to her, the gossiper will hurt, and maybe lose forever, a good friend, not to mention earning herself an untrustworthy reputation.

Have you ever been guilty of being a blabbermouth yourself? If so, just remember, no matter how juicy the information, spilling a friend's secret just isn't worth it. You may lose her trust, or worse, your entire friendship with her. You could even damage your other relationships as well because once other friends see how untrustworthy you are, they may cut you out of the loop completely to keep their own secrets safe. Or they may decide to teach you a lesson, like Jenny and her friends from California did:

Jenny and her friends were tired of Alison spreading their secrets. Whenever one of them told her anything, everyone else in their group would have heard about it by the end of the day. So to get back at her they started to tell her wild and outrageous lies about everyone and everything. Then whenever Alison would spill one of these silly secrets to their group, everyone would burst out laughing and make fun of her. It wasn't the nicest way to tame a blabbermouth, but after a while Alison learned to keep what she heard to herself.

Reach out

Quick: When are your closest friends' birthdays? If you don't know, find out right now and write the dates down somewhere you won't forget. It's not like you have to memorize the Declaration of Independence, just the birth dates of your most important friends in the world! Then when their birthdays come around you'll be ready to e-mail a card or call to let them know you remembered. It's nice, too, to give a friend an inexpensive gift or token of your friendship from the heart.

This stuff is important! Nothing is sadder than losing a friend over a forgotten birthday, missed party, or because you were too busy keeping track of whose turn it was to call whom to actually pick up the phone! Whether your friend is in the classroom across the hall or living in a different state, keep in touch by e-mail, snail mail, or telephone and remember those special days.

What if it seems like you're the one making all the effort? Well, is your friend purposely ignoring you or just lousy at keeping in touch? If she really doesn't want to talk to you, you'll catch on quickly — her mom will say she's busy every time you call and she'll never have time for you no matter what day you try to make plans. On the other hand, if your friend is just a flake but sounds genuinely happy every time you call, you have to decide if this friendship is worth the trouble. If the answer is yes, then you'll just have to accept her ways. Stop nagging her every two seconds to call you and just take it on yourself to make the effort. If she's a good friend, she's worth it.

Smile

Given the choice, you'd probably choose a happy-go-lucky friend over someone who constantly complains and makes you miserable. We all would. That doesn't mean you can't ever be in a bad mood, since everyone goes through ups and downs. But if you spend every day putting friends down and snapping their heads off, you're quickly going to find yourself alone.

Try putting a positive spin on things and becoming the kind of person you'd like to know — someone who doesn't spread rumors or gossip about people behind their backs and isn't a total pessimist. In other words, be the kindest, nicest, funniest person you can be.

After all, compliments and smiles are free and they can cause you to get so much back in return. So go ahead and say something nice to everyone you meet or smile at kids you'd like to get to know. You'll be pleasantly surprised at how well people react to your sunny attitude. Of course, you want to keep it sincere because people can spot fake flattery a mile away. But making kids feel good about themselves is the quickest way to a friendship.

Lean on me

Your friends are sure to have days when it seems like nothing goes right. Their alarm clock didn't go off, the morning milk was sour, they missed the school bus, a teacher was super-strict. Times like that, the most important thing you can do is give your support. Your friends are probably counting on you to be the bright spot in their otherwise horrible, miserable day.

Even if you don't immediately feel appreciated, your thoughtfulness won't go unnoticed and is sure to mean a lot to your friends.

Danielle, from Montana, still remembers how her best friend came through in a tough time. "When my grandpa died, she sent me a sympathy card and called him 'our grandpa' since we've known each other since preschool. Knowing she cared made me feel better."

Unfortunately, some girls can be fair-weather friends. That means they're always around to enjoy the fun times, like sleepovers and movie nights, but then, at the first sign of trouble, they're nowhere to be found. A true friend will stick around through good and bad, offering a laugh, a hug, a shoulder to lean on, a sympathetic ear — whatever is needed.

Both you and your best friend have every right to expect you will be there for each other — that's what friendship is all about. Help should only be a phone call away. Don't accept anything less.

Fun stuff to do for your friend
Why don't you . . .
- Bake her chocolate chip cookies.
- Make a mix tape of her favorite music.
- Get to know her better by looking through her family photo albums.
- Make a memory box filled with personal notes, pictures, and ticket stubs from

places you've been or things you've done together.

- Celebrate her half birthday, 182½ days after the real deal.
- Lend her something — like your favorite sweater or a good book — you know she's been dying to borrow.
- Send her a postcard, e-mail, or "just because" card just because she's your friend and just to say hi.
- Give her a manicure.
- Treat her to snapshots of the two of you at an instant photo booth.
- Make her a beaded bracelet or necklace.

Things we do together that show what great buds we are

"We get way hyper, which means we do psycho dances around the house, have food fights, water fights, put on fashion shows, and do anything else that comes to mind. Everything we do is a cool, fun experience."

Kate, Oregon

"We make sure we go on at least one shopping trip a month; it's like a religion for us. You know, the girl bonding thing is a must!"

Jamie, Ontario, Canada

"We go to our neighborhood park, swing on the swings, and just take a break from our stressful lives."

Leslie, Louisiana

"We talk. I love to let all my previously un-expressed feelings out to my most trusted best bud. We talk about celebrities, boys, clothes, movies, friends, perfect lives, embar-rassing moments, the latest magazines and TV shows."

Caroline, Washington

"We give each other makeovers."

Kirstin, Saskatchewan, Canada

"We have a gab-fest about anything and every-thing that comes to mind . . . especially boys!"

Jessica, Oklahoma

"We go to the mall and try on all these funky clothes that we would never buy."

Shelly, Texas

Best friends are great because . . .
". . . you can pig out in front of them and not feel uncomfortable, like you do around boys,

and you can go on and on about your latest crush and they're always there to listen."

Elizabeth, Georgia

". . . you can talk to them about things you wouldn't want to share with your parents or a boy."

Crystal Ann, California

". . . you can be crazy and comfortable with them."

Ashley, Virginia

". . . the really good ones you can tell anything. You don't have to worry about what you're doing or how you dress — they don't care. And you don't have to worry about what they're thinking because you usually know."

Nicole, Missouri

". . . you can act any way you want around them without feeling embarrassed."

Jay, Pennsylvania

". . . no matter how serious or stupid the matter, they'll always be there for you. They're a soul to talk to and a shoulder to lean on."

Rachel, North Carolina

". . . they listen when all you want to do is cry."

Vikki, Pennsylvania

". . . you can go on and on about how great Isaac Hanson looked at the Video Music Awards. Boys just wouldn't put up with that."

Michelle, California

". . . they're there with you through it all. Even if you're just having a bad hair day, they cheer you up completely."

Natalie, Missouri

". . . they're there for you all the time and you can talk about girl problems that you can't talk about with boys."

Katie, Massachusetts

". . . you can be yourself around them since you're more comfortable with them and you can do things that you both find fun that you wouldn't do with anyone else."

Katie, Missouri

". . . they tell you what they really think about you (in a nice way) and don't care how you look."

Michelle, Texas

Chapter Four

The Friendship Game

How Many Friends Are Enough?

If a new girl walked into your classroom tomorrow, would you make a mental note to talk to her at lunchtime or would you think "I don't really need to meet this girl because I've already got a bunch of friends"? If you choose to ignore the new girl, you're missing out on a great opportunity to become a better person yourself. How's that? It's hard to grow as a person or learn anything new if you're not open to new friends and experiences.

For example, if you chat with the new girl, you might find out she's from a part of the country you don't know much about and by talking to her you could learn something new. Or, maybe she's got a pet rabbit, writes great short stories, or is looking for someone to teach her how to in-line skate. The more girls you meet, the more ideas and interests you'll be exposed to.

Just imagine that every day at school, for a whole year, your class studied division and spelling all day long. That's it — just two subjects. No history, no geography, no science, no art, no literature. You'd be able to divide any number and spell a zillion words but you'd be ignorant about a whole load of other things.

Think of your friends the same way. You can have a favorite friend but that shouldn't stop you from meeting as many people as you possibly can. Brette might love horseback riding while Melissa likes drawing in her sketchbook. You might pick up both of their hobbies or decide that neither is for you but at least the next time someone invites you to go riding you'll know a little about what you're getting yourself into.

While it's great to be friendly, that doesn't mean you should try to make every girl you meet into your soul mate. You can end up spreading yourself too thin by trying to be everyone's best friend. And if you are spending your time trying to get to know absolutely everyone, you'll never really have the time to get close to a special pal or two.

Casual friendships are fun and take less time and effort to maintain than close friendships. Casual friends are great to invite to your party or to go to the mall with, but you might feel a little uncomfortable telling them your deepest, darkest secrets. That's because casual friends are more likely to come into and go out of your life as you change schools, develop new interests, and get older. And that's OK — they're not meant to be your forever friends. They're there to fill out your social group and bring some fun and laughter into your life. And who knows, along the way two of you may click and become much closer.

Friends make you feel better

Feeling down? Better call a friend. Of course you already know being with your friends makes you happy, but did you know that there's now some serious scientific evidence that proves bonding time also makes you healthier? It's true!

A study of stressed-out college medical students showed that people who rated high on the loneliness scale were much more likely to become sick than students who had a strong network of friends and family.

According to the study from the Ohio State University Medical Center, bumming over friendship blues weakens your immune system. Meanwhile, having good friends toughens your resistance to disease.

So be thankful your friends are around to help you feel your best. And if you do catch a cold, pop some vitamin C and call a friend or two. You'll feel better in the morning.

Am I abandoning my old friends?

"Make new friends but keep the old; one is silver and the other gold."

Girl Scout saying

Sometimes making new friends can be tricky because it can cause your old friends to feel like you're abandoning them. But there's nothing wrong with the introduction of a new face into your group as long as you're careful not to hurt anyone's feelings. You might want to reassure your best friend that you haven't changed how you feel about her. Explain that you just think this new girl is really nice and would fit in well with your circle.

Of course, it's possible your old pal might really have a reason to be upset. Like, are you too busy hanging with your new bud to talk to her on the phone anymore? Do you immediately turn to your new pal when the teacher asks you to pick a partner? If so, you can't blame your other friend for feeling hurt and you owe her an explanation. If your feelings *have* changed and you'd really rather spend all your time with your new friend, then you're going to have to do the honorable thing and tell your old friend. She may blame herself for your change of heart and start coming down hard on herself, so it's up to you to let her know you still like her, but that you just don't feel as close to her as you used to.

Share-a-friend

Sometimes the shoe is on the other foot and it's your best friend (not you) who wants to bail. In a perfect world, you'd never get jealous. You wouldn't care if another friend of your best friend was smarter, nicer, or prettier. And you wouldn't care if your best friend wanted to spend Saturday afternoon with someone else. But that's not the way it works. Chances are, the thought of her having another best friend makes you feel sick to your stomach.

It could (and does) happen — suddenly your true-blue pal starts hanging with someone else. But if you can't understand why your friend would want to hang out with anyone else when she's got you, it's time for an attitude adjustment. You can't cut your friend off from the outside world and keep her all to yourself (even if you'd like to). You're going to have to accept her other friends or risk losing her friendship.

Jenny from California explained why she thinks having a couple of best friends is better than just one. "My two best friends are different. One of them is really wild and crazy and is always coming up with fun stuff for us to do. The other one is a really good listener; whenever I have a problem I really feel like she understands me. I love them both but sometimes I need one more than the other."

Ultimately, the harder you cling to your friend, the more she's going to pull away. Instead, give her some room to breathe and treat her new friends graciously. This will convince her that you understand and really want what's best for her.

But how will I ever keep busy?
If you and your friend are no longer joined at the hip, now's your chance to develop your own interests outside the friendship. Like, maybe your friend would always insist on renting comedies whenever she came over? Well, now you can rent something *you* really want to see, like a scary suspense movie. Or sign up for a club or after-school activity you're interested in that you know she'd never want to join. The more hobbies and interests you're involved with, the more you'll learn, the more interesting you'll be, and the more new potential pals you'll meet.

What else can I do?
Suggest you'd like to get to know your friend's new friends better. After all, no one said you couldn't *all* be friends. Invite your BFF and her new pals over after school or sit with them at lunch. If your best friend thinks these girls are special, chances are you'll like them, too. After all, she had the great taste to pick you as a friend, right?

But don't forget about making your own new friends. There's no need for you to be alone when your best friend is busy. This is the

best time for you to pursue other relationships. And these new friends might just bring
out good qualities in you that you didn't even
realize you had!

Stuck in the middle

"Two of my friends got in a fight and now they
won't leave me alone. They refuse to speak
to each other and make me pass nasty mes-
sages back and forth. I'm getting really sick of
this."

Dana, California

Being caught between two feuding friends is
no fun. Whether it's an old pal who doesn't
approve of your new friendship or two of
your friends who don't get along, you're likely
to be dragged into the fight even if it has
nothing to do with you. Each will encourage
you to insult or ignore the other person.

Your best bet when stuck in the middle is to
take yourself out of the conflict. Let each
friend know how much you like her but insist
you won't take sides. The problem is between
them and they're just going to have to solve it
on their own. Your refusal to get involved or
make a big deal over it might even get them to
realize that their disagreement and problems

are actually not worth all the trouble. Who knows, maybe they'll work it out and become friends again. But even if they don't, by not getting involved you will have avoided hurting anyone's feelings and will hopefully be able to keep both friendships.

Help! I'm being left behind: When three's a crowd

Lisa liked to include both her friends — Samantha, her school pal, and Michelle, her next-door neighbor — in her weekend plans. Whenever she threw a sleepover or rented a movie, she'd make sure to invite them both.

But then Samantha and Michelle started making plans together that didn't include her. The one time Lisa confronted them about it, they just said she was imagining things. They claimed Lisa was always busy when they planned things or else they definitely would have invited her along. But since then, nothing had changed. Samantha and Michelle continued to see each other without including Lisa.

Lisa felt like she must've done something awful for Samantha and Michelle to have cut her out. But most likely they just discovered they had more in common with each other than they did with her. Being left out is a horrible feeling but there are some things you can do to get over the pain:

- Talk to your friend. Tell her that she has hurt your feelings and ask her to explain what happened and how she's feeling about it. It's possible she may not realize that she's been leaving you out or that you'd take it so personally.
- If it's quite clear that your friend is more interested in someone else, don't beat yourself up about it. It's a fact of life that people change and grow apart.
- Don't change just to fit in or to try to save a friendship that's probably not meant to last. For example, if a friend is going through a boy-crazy phase, don't fake the same feelings. You'll eventually get sick of being someone you're not.
- Move on. If the friendship is over, it's time for you to find new friends who will enjoy your company as much as your old friend once did.

Chapter Five
True-Blue Buds

A Checklist

Here are thirty things a friend can do that show she really cares and that she's truly a good friend. Do any of these scenarios sound familiar? The more of these that describe your friend, the better bud she is.

1. She doesn't tell anyone that the ugly pair of tan undies on the gym floor dropped out of your bag.

2. She's on constant lookout for anything potentially embarrassing to you, like bits of food stuck in your teeth or stains on your shirt.

3. She's the only person who actually takes the time to talk to your dad when he answers the phone and even laughs at his lame jokes.

4. She makes you feel better after you wipe out in the school hallway in front of your latest crush.

5. She sticks up for you, even if it means going against the most popular kids at school.

6. She stays up all night making cupcakes with you for a bake sale after you forgot to plan ahead.

7. She keeps your deepest, darkest secrets.

8. She doesn't go ballistic when, unplanned, you both wear the same outfit to school — in fact, she thinks it just proves you two are meant to be best friends.

9. She always helps you study for science tests, since she's more confident in the subject than you are.

10. She doesn't cancel plans with you, even when she gets a better offer.

11. She doesn't tell you she's too busy to talk on the phone.

12. She wouldn't dream of flirting with your crush, even if the two of them are good friends.

13. She doesn't try to outdo you when you succeed at something.

14. She takes the blame when the teacher catches the two of you passing notes in class, even though you were the one who wrote the note.

15. She remembers all your allergies and makes sure nothing sets you off.

16. She's even more excited than you are when something good happens to you.

17. She makes sure her mom picks up a bag of Double Stuf Oreo cookies every time you come over 'cause she knows they're your favorites.

18. She brings you your homework when you're out sick and then spends hours telling you everything that happened in school that day.

19. She doesn't get mad at you when you don't call her right back.

20. She puts up with your weird moods, candy cravings, and odd behavior during full moons.

21. She tells you the truth when you ask.

22. She softens the truth when you don't really want to hear it.

23. She lends you her favorite sweater and doesn't bug you to return it even after you've had it for weeks.

24. She remembers your mom's birthday.

25. She canceled plans and rushed over to your house when your cat died.

26. She calls and tells you stuff before letting anyone else know.

27. She agrees to get her ears pierced first 'cause you're afraid it'll hurt too much.

28. She splits her sandwich with you when you forget your lunch and the only thing the cafeteria is serving is mystery meat.

29. She doesn't complain when you want to go to a movie she's already seen.

30. She can make her point and still let you get in the last word.

Chapter Six

How Well Do You Know Your (Best) Friend?

Fifty Fun Questions to Ask Yourself

Are you really as close to your best friend as you think? Quick, what's her favorite color, favorite movie, favorite ice-cream flavor? Here are fifty things you absolutely should know about your best friend (and that she should know about you)!

1. Who's her favorite Hollywood hottie?

2. What movie could she watch a million times and never get sick of?

3. What's the best book she's ever read?

4. Who's her favorite author?

5. What CD has she worn out replaying over and over?

6. What TV show would she never miss?

7. Which TV actor does she think is the cutest?

8. Which TV actress does she admire?

9. What's her favorite outfit?

10. What's her shoe size?

11. What's her favorite color?

12. Where's her favorite place to shop?

13. Is she a chocoholic?

14. What's her favorite food?

15. Which ice-cream flavor makes her melt?

16. What type of candy does she love?

17. What's her favorite pick from the lunch line?

18. What cafeteria food makes her gag?

19. Is she a dog or cat person?

20. What cartoon makes her laugh the most?

21. What's her favorite thing to do on week-ends?

22. What type of flowers would she like to receive?

23. What are her pet peeves?

24. What's her favorite saying?

25. What does she think are her best and worst qualities?

26. When's her birthday?

27. What is her favorite subject in school? Her least favorite?

28. Who is her favorite teacher of all time?

29. Who makes her life miserable at school?

30. What sport does she love to play?

31. Which athlete is her heroine?

32. Does she think she's too tall, too small, too thin, too fat?

33. Which of her relatives is she closest to?

34. What's the most embarrassing thing that's ever happened to her?

35. What's her astrological sign?

36. Does she read her horoscope every day?

37. Does she have a recurring dream? If so, what is it?

38. If she could change anything about her life, what would it be?

39. What's been the best moment of her life so far?

40. Where did she grow up?

41. Where would she go if she could travel anywhere in the world?

42. What does she worry about the most?

43. What could make her instantly happy?

44. Is having money important to her?

45. Is she a spiritual person?

46. Does she believe in reincarnation? If so, what would she like to be in her next life?

47. What's her religion?

48. What does she want to be when she gets older?

49. Who's made the biggest impact on her life?

50. If the world were to end tomorrow, what would she like to spend her last day doing?

Chapter Seven
When Friends Fight

When asked if they fight with their friends, a lot of girls answer, *"Oh, we never fight."* While that may sound wonderful, it isn't necessarily a good thing (or even true). Fighting isn't all about screaming and insulting each other — it's about letting the other person know that you disagree with her opinion or behavior or that something she said or did hurt you.

After all, no matter how well you get along with your best friend, there are sure to be times she upsets you. Hopefully, it doesn't end up being a big deal. If you're confident about your relationship with her, you should be able to let her know what the problem is, talk about it, and then move on. But if you don't speak up and just swallow the hurt or anger, either out of a false sense of loyalty or because you're afraid your friend will get mad and abandon you, then you're in for trouble.

Your bottled-up feelings will swell up like soda bubbles in a can and eventually explode. You could end up saying mean, hurtful things to your friend that could completely destroy your friendship. It's a lot harder to patch up a broken friendship than it is to talk through a problem. You should always share your feelings from the very beginning.

How to fight fair

Do you know how to handle yourself when your friend does something that upsets you? We're not talking about anything outrageous (there's more about that later), but what if your pal borrowed a sweater and returned it with a stain?

Would you refuse to speak to her, or would you let it slide but vow never to lend her anything ever again? Both actions are pretty drastic. After all, it's hardly worth ruining your friendship over a measly sweater, nor do you want her to think everything's fine but then end up freaking out the next time she asks to borrow something.

The best way to handle a situation like this would be to calmly let her know that you're upset about the sweater, but avoid making it into something bigger. Don't try to make her feel even smaller by saying, "*I knew you'd do something like this. You're such a slob.*" By explaining, not blaming, the two of you can talk things over and hopefully resolve the problem.

If your friend values your friendship, she'll apologize and offer to clean or replace the sweater. But if she refuses to accept any responsibility, or even gets mad at you for bringing it up, then that's a much tougher situation to handle. If she continually refuses to take responsibility for her actions and takes advantage of your friendship, you'll have to reconsider whether this is a friend you want to have. Or you could discuss the situation with an adult who might be able to give you some helpful advice.

By dealing with friendship problems calmly, you can get everything off your chest and prevent future blowups — all without hurting your friend's feelings. Screaming at friends usually just puts them on the defensive and can end up ruining your relationships.

Forgiveness
Say your friend blabs a secret she swore she'd take to her grave and then later asks for your

forgiveness. Do you need to forgive her right away? Absolutely not. Betraying a trust is a very serious thing and not easily or quickly forgotten. You should take as much time as you need to calm down. But once you decide to talk to your friend about what she did, make sure you get everything off your chest. Because if you don't, the problem will never really go away. At the same time, once you've forgiven someone, you can't keep bringing up what she did or keep saying over and over, "*I can't believe you did that to me.*"

Once you do start talking to your friend, explain how her actions hurt you. Tell her she let you down and betrayed your trust and that she'll have to earn back that trust. If you think there's something specific she could do to help patch things up, tell her what it is.

It's also important that you give her a chance to be heard. Give her the opportunity to explain how she ended up making such a huge mistake. Hopefully, she'll feel awful about what she did, give you a supersincere apology, and promise never to do again whatever it was she did. When you're ready, forgive her and then drop it. Holding a grudge over your friend's mistake will only make you both suffer even more!

Letting off steam

Suppose you've already forgiven your friend for something she did but just can't seem to get over her blunder. Here are a few ways to get out that anger without taking it out on your pal and possibly ending the friendship:

- Get some exercise. Put your energy into running around the block or kicking a soccer ball. It'll help you cool off while getting your mind off your problems.
- Shut the door and scream. Release your anger by pounding on your pillow and screaming at the mirror. (You might want to warn Mom and Dad in advance.) Better you hit your pillow than your friend.
- Put your feelings down on paper. Get some satisfaction by writing your friend a note describing how mad you are, then tear it up. No one ever needs to know about your poison-pen letter but getting all your anger out will help you let it go.

When it's your fault

What if *you're* the one who messed up and now your friend won't talk to you — what do you do? Well, first and foremost, apologize. Immediately. Accept full responsibility for what you did and don't make things any worse by pointing fingers at her. After all, an apology followed by *"But it's your fault I did it in the first place"* won't help matters a bit.

What not to say to a friend

In fact, there are several things you should never say to a friend even if you want to share everything with her. Honesty is one thing, squashing her with the brutal truth is another. Avoid saying:

"Yup, you messed up." Don't remind a friend that she's done wrong when she already feels awful about a mistake she's made.

"I have to cancel our plans on Friday 'cause Kathy's having a party." Don't cancel plans with a friend just because you've gotten a better offer.

"That's too bad but wait till you hear what happened to me." Don't try to top her story with one of yours.

"I liked your hair better before the cut." Don't try to make her feel bad about something that's already done and *beyond her control*.

"You always do this." Keep the words *always* and *never* out of your conversations.

Patching things up

How do you avoid breaking up with friends for good? Here's what some girls have to say about how they handled their fights and were able to save their friendships:

"My best friend and I have been in a few major fights that have threatened our friendship. We've learned when it's time to back off and give the other person some space."

Elizabeth, Massachusetts

"I've gotten in little fights with my friends before. Basically, when it's something small, I give them a few days to blow off steam and we both think about what we've done wrong; then we call each other to patch things up."

Vicky, Ohio

"I asked my teacher and other friends for a lot of advice when a friend and I had a fight."

Elana, Ohio

"We got over it and decided to forget about the silly incident. We were going to have to see each other for the next four years so why not get along?"

Melissa, Pennsylvania

"The way I make up for fights that seem silly is to call up my friend and say, 'I'm sorry, I was in a bad mood and I feel like a pig. I was wondering if you'd like to crash at my house on Saturday.' A true friend will accept your apology and if she's free maybe bring a few flicks over. Troubles fly away when you watch a cute friendship flick like *Now and Then*."

Caroline, Washington

"I used to have a lot of fights with my best friend. After a serious fight we stopped talking for four months. Then we worked out that we shouldn't be best friends, just close ones."

Shelly, Texas

Looking out for bad-for-you friends

"I don't know why, but I'm a target for everyone to pick on. But I never thought I'd have to put up with that sort of stuff from my best friend. She stuck a KICK ME sign on my back. She calls me names like 'baby feet' because I have small feet, and 'skinny and flat' because I'm pretty thin. But the thing that made me lose it was when she stuck a wet Oreo to my forehead. We got into an argument and now she's mad at me for being mad at her."

Anonymous, Wisconsin

Are all friendship fights worth fixing? Absolutely not. When a friend crosses the line and does something that's not just insensitive but downright mean, you might want to consider saying "so long," or at least taking a long, hard look at your friendship. After all, friends should be supportive and have good intentions — someone who's often mean and hurtful to you is *not* a friend.

Maybe the problem isn't that one of your friends is mean to you, but that you've been feeling totally out of touch with her lately. Perhaps she has started hanging with a bad crowd that thinks doing stupid stuff like shoplifting is cool. Or maybe she's always been kind of shallow but since you've always been her only friend you never wanted to give up on her. Only now it seems like she's never there for you and when she is around, you become the butt of her jokes and temper tantrums.

There are many things that can cause a friendship to sour. When the bad really starts to outweigh the good, it's time to think about moving on. Ask yourself these questions: Do most of your conversations with her focus on how much fun you had in the past? Do you often think you'd be a happier person without her? Are you clinging to the friendship because you don't really have any other friends? If you answer yes to any of these questions, you should put some serious thought into ending this going-nowhere friendship.

This isn't about giving up on a friend who deserves a second chance. This is about a friend who is so negative, mean, or self-destructive that she's hurting you in the process. It may be hard, but in these instances you need to admit this friendship is over and move on or risk getting dragged down with her. If you are concerned that she might really hurt herself or get into trouble, and if you feel guilty for abandoning her when she's down, you can always turn to an adult you trust for advice on how to handle the situation. You still should separate yourself from her, though, because if you don't there's always the chance you'll get in too deep and be headed for trouble, too.

Danger ahead

Here are some warning signs that your friend-ship might be headed for trouble:

- You feel insecure every time she's around.
- You make excuses to get out of spending time with her.
- You complain about her to other friends or family members.
- You squabble over silly stuff that wouldn't normally bother you.
- You don't feel like you can be completely honest with her.
- You disapprove of many things she does.
- When you look at her, it's like looking at a stranger.
- You feel like your problems with her are ruining the rest of your life.

How to say good-bye

If you think you'd be better off without this friend, ease her out of your life. Let the phone calls drop off. Avoid making plans together. Spend more time with good-for-you friends who aren't part of the same social circle. Distance will finish off what you started.

Once she's gone, give yourself time to mourn. You don't have to jump right back in the game if you've just ended a meaningful friendship. Spend some time thinking about how things went wrong. This way you'll know what to look for in a new friend and hopefully you'll be able to recognize the warning signals of a bad friendship.

Chapter Eight

"What Tore Us Apart" Stories

Whether your friendship slowly fades away or you and your "friend" have a horrible fight, sometimes breaking up is the only choice. Of course, there's always the chance of patching things up but, sadly, there's no guarantee.

"I broke up with a friend because she was a real snob. She was always competitive and had to be the best and she put other people down. I told her how I felt and how I thought she was being really mean. She said that she didn't care what I thought."

Jane, Illinois

"My best friend started to hang out exclusively with another one of our friends. They

63

ignored me and talked about me behind my back. Every once in a while she would act like she was my best friend again and then on other days she'd act like she was too good to talk to me. After a while she e-mailed me and apologized. We're friends again but things will never be the same."

Elana, Ohio

"I had one friend who always wanted all my attention. No matter where I went or what I was doing she was there tagging along. It bugged me so much because she felt like she constantly had to be by my side. It got to the point where she told my other friends lies about me so that they would stop being friends with me; then it would be just me and her. Her plan didn't succeed and we're not friends anymore."

Jessica, Oklahoma

"One of my friends has a boyfriend and she gets mad when people talk to him. I was in the same math group with him and we'd talk about movies or music so now she won't talk to me anymore."

Caroline, Washington

"When I was in fourth grade there was a new student in my best friend's class. This new student became friends with my best friend but she didn't want to include me in anything. She forbade my friend to see me or talk to me. My friend and I didn't talk for that whole school year. But eventually we got back together. I think your true friends will always stick by you and won't ever let you down."

Elizabeth, Massachusetts

"Most of the time my old friends and I drift apart over the summer when we don't see each other. But then we usually get back together the next time we're in the same class."

Vicky, Ohio

"I was hanging out with these two girls and I ended up breaking them apart. It all happened because the girl I usually hung out with got mad when I tried to spend some time with her other friend. We got in a huge fight and now none of us are really close anymore."

Shelly, Texas

"My best friend of four years suddenly grew apart from me and I just had to let go. It bothered me but there wasn't much I could do."

Michelle, Oregon

Chapter Nine

How to Be Friends with a Boy

Or What's So Cool about Boys?

This book is mainly about you and your girl pals but that doesn't mean you can't have friends who are boys — it's just that friendship with a boy can be a little more complicated. When you were little, it didn't matter to you if the kid next door was a boy — if he had the best video game collection on the block, then you wanted to play together every day anyway. But now that you're older, you may find that you've grown apart from boys. Sometimes it's your own feelings and different interests that come between the two of you; other times, it's what other friends think.

As you get closer to the age that boys and girls start dating, you may feel nervous or uncomfortable about talking to boys. With a lot of your friends, all they seem to do around boys is giggle. And the boys themselves act so weird sometimes — roughhousing, telling stupid jokes, acting gross — that you may wonder why *anyone* would want to be friends with them. But don't let other girls' awkwardness or the fact that some boys are jerks stop you from making friends with those boys you think are nice.

'Cause boys aren't just potential date material — they're often cool, interesting people you should get to know. They're not the same as (or a substitute for) girlfriends, of course, but you'd probably be surprised to learn how much you have in common. Your schoolwork, for one thing, and music, movies, books, and who knows what else!

But you don't have to share all the same interests to enjoy the company of boys. What makes boys different from you and your girlfriends is what makes them special. After all, if every friend were a carbon copy of you, things would be mighty boring! Since boys often have very different emotional reactions to things than girls do, you can get a totally different perspective on situations from them. Here's the deal — boys tend to be more action-oriented than girls. When they've got a goal to focus on — like finishing their science fair project or winning a football game — they perform better because there's only one thing they have to concentrate on. Girls are able to jump from one topic or activity to another more easily without losing track of what they were doing in the first place. Neither of these qualities is better than the other, just different.

Lisa, from New York, finds hanging out with a boy who's her friend more relaxing than being with some of her girlfriends. "I like hanging out with Dave because what you see is what you get. I'm not always worrying about what he's thinking or feeling because he's totally honest and doesn't keep secrets." Sometimes girls aren't as straightforward and easy to read as most boys.

And it's not just girls who want friends of the opposite sex. Ryan, from California, definitely sees the pros in having friends who are girls. "It's great because the conversations are totally different; you don't always have to talk about football and baseball all the time."

Becoming friends with boys

If you have an older or younger brother or have a good friend who's a boy, you already have a head start when it comes time to make new guy friends. But if you've never really spent much time with boys, becoming friends with them might seem intimidating. But it doesn't have to be that difficult — or that scary.

If there's a certain boy who you think would be tons of fun to hang out with, look around and see if you have any mutual friends. If you do have a mutual friend, it'll be easier to get to know him better because you'll have more opportunities to talk to him; it'll be easier to approach him if you've already met before or at least have seen each other around. Try planning group activities with kids you both know so neither of you feels uncomfortable.

Or maybe there's a boy in your class who seems nice and who you think would make a good friend. You may know him well enough to say hi but how do you get to be actual *friends* with him? This may surprise you, but you really don't need to do anything different from what you'd do to become friends with a girl. So follow the same tips from the rest of this book: Be friendly, open, and interested, and it shouldn't be too difficult from there.

Will this boy think you have a crush on him? Not if you don't act like you do. If you can just be yourself and act like you would around your girlfriends, he shouldn't get the wrong idea. Just use your common sense when it comes to making plans. Asking him to watch TV after school is a totally different scenario than inviting him to the movies — just the two of you — on the weekend.

Getting involved in coed activities is another way of making friends of the opposite sex. Sign up for after-school clubs or jump in if you're invited to play a round of volleyball with a mixed group. Try to avoid hanging in strictly "girls-only" cliques. Think about it from a boy's point of view — he's just as nervous about saying hi to you in front of all your friends as you would be in front of all his friends.

Go for it
If you ever wonder what a boy might be thinking when you approach him, then check out these responses:

"I like it when a girl is just being herself, being cool and nice to everyone, not acting like she's trying to get a guy."

Tony, California

"You can't be shy. Just go up and talk to him."

Nick, New Jersey

"I'm kind of shy myself so if a girl came up and talked to me I'd think that was really cool."

Daniel, Quebec, Canada

"I like a girl who can be straightforward and honest with me."

Chris, Arizona

How to stay friends

Maybe you're already close to a boy or you'd like to spend some more time with the boy who sits next to you in class but the constant teasing is driving you crazy. You can't even have a conversation with a boy without your friends thinking you have a crush on him. What gives? Take a look around — the girls who tease you the most probably don't have any friends who are boys. They probably can't understand why you'd ever want to be friends with a boy and what you enjoy about his company because they just don't have any similar experiences.

Your friends might even be jealous of how comfortable you are dealing with boys. By trying to make you feel uncomfortable, too, they may be trying to bring you to their level in order to make themselves feel better. The next time someone gives you grief for being friends with a boy, don't deny it or try to change the subject. Face them and say, "Yeah, we're friends, so what?" The quickest way to shut people up is to let them know that they have no effect on you.

But what if your (boy) friend can't deal with the extra attention and starts pulling away? Caroline and Josh spent a lot of time together on the weekends because their parents were friends. They always had a good time, but back at school, with his buddies, he wouldn't even acknowledge her.

Peer pressure is a really powerful thing and your friend might not be strong enough to withstand it. Eric, from California, says, "If I was having a conversation with a girl and my friends showed up, I'd definitely start acting differently, because what happens between us is personal."

If you're friends with a boy and this is the way your relationship is, then as long as you don't mind a part-time friendship that changes depending on the day of the week or who's around, then it's fine. In time, he may become a true-blue friend. For now, just enjoy his company as is.

Conclusion
Friends Forever

Anything that's worthwhile takes time and energy. True friendship won't happen overnight, but you've already taken a step in the right direction by reading this book. (Maybe you didn't even make it through the book before you felt you just had to call her to say hi.) It's just as important to understand what can hurt your friendship as it is to know how you can make things better.

Of course, the fun stuff, like making cookies with her or having a sleepover, is always going to be easier. But listening to her, understanding her, and forgiving her are the things that will firmly establish your friendship.

Why is this all your responsibility? It's not. But the thing is, you can't control your friend's behavior, you can only control your own actions. Therefore, it's up to you to make the best of the friendship that you can. Don't worry. Your friend will likely be quick to catch on to your extra effort and do the same for you. It's really true: You get out of a relationship what you put into it.

Hopefully, this book will have inspired you to think about and do more for your friendships. You can probably come up with a zillion more ways to let your best friend know you care — and write a book of your own!

Friendship is a wonderful thing. It lets you know you're not alone in this crazy world. You owe it to your friend — and to yourself — to work on developing a friendship that's really special.